Bold, Assertive
and Tender

Jeremy Vasquez

You know how it is. You pick up a book, flip to the dedication page and find that, once again, the author has dedicated a book to someone else and not you.

Not this time.

You are as much a part of the pages as the hands that went into writing on them. For every author is nothing more than a cassette player, placed at designated points of the world to record personal experiences and reflect society. It's ironic that the greatest torment led me to do what I love. Thank you to everyone that convinced me to trust the calling-- those who disheartened me in the face of overwhelming odds and those who encouraged me with words of affirmation. It all happened *for* me, not *to* me. It was the gravitational pull of the universe that brought you here and I hope it's the tidal waves of quiet comfort that you are about to experience that keep you returning. This compilation of work would not have been possible without the magic of the human condition and the unconditional love of an immigrant from Trinidad and Tobago who taught me to be greater than what I suffer.

Author's Note

Before you get started, I would like to thank my friend and amazing editor, Alyssa Marie Vega, for her assistance and for being a helping hand in the production of this book. Without her commitment, this would not have been possible. I would also like to thank my graphic designer and personal confidant, Preet Brar, for putting my vision to fruition; and fellow kindred spirit, Natalie Corazon, for taking the time to go through my work and elevate its impact. I was inspired to write this book when I returned from my trip to Europe earlier this year where I visited Italy and Paris. Upon my layover in New York, a friend asked, "Do you still write?" I made excuses and responded "No." As I traveled through various countries I came across people with different points of view, saw things that startled me, felt emotions I never felt before. It was a profound experience and I returned quite a different person than the one who left. I thought about the conversation I had with my friend in New York, and I realized a wormhole had been opened; I knew I needed to revisit my first love while she still lives--writing.

Bold

1 | How Does Royalty Stomp in the Mud with Grace?

I watched you. You convinced me at an early age that colored girls had no right to sorrow. Bessie sang the blues, so you wouldn't have to relate. Nina was misunderstood so you wouldn't be strange fruit today. Your whole being is provocative. Your very existence is defiant. Straighteners were created to keep you in line. Barbies were made to mock you. Your whole life, society has expected you to submit while all instinct has ever taught you is to survive.

Have you ever looked at a tiger and thought you ought to cover it up? You did no such thing. I have gazed upon your Africanness without apology. You are throes of a beauty renaissance. How could you ever expect caucasian counterparts not to be "confused" by your afro and its unapologetic nature? Nothing about your locs are dreadful. How many ignorant slurs has the curl of your hair had to endure? You've been a petting zoo to girls and boys of parents whose parents treated our ancestors like circus animals of The Ringling Brothers. The satire. You are Django unchained. You are Lauryn Hill unplugged. You are a descendant from where accents are as thick as figures; your skin is as rich as chocolate, and our crowns were stitched in while we were still in the womb kicking.

Do lions lose sleep over the opinion of sheep? You haven't. Your
curves have caused traffic jams since the invention of motor
vehicles. Whether the media has labeled you BBW or plus size,
you have hidden in the narrow shade of bikinis custom made for
the anorexics too long. There is no secret to Victoria, only
circumference and your pie is far too immaculate to fit into society's
norms. Your birthing hips dance to the rhythm of drums, your waist
level is not eye-level to men with weak appetites. Models were
made for modeling; thick women were made for cuddling.

How can I be an artist and not reflect the times? I can't. They've
made us spite you. They've carved stereotypes into our scalps
since adolescence. Disney didn't believe Queens came in shades
of your complexion until I was in college, at which point Princess
Tiana was nothing more than an animorph. They've conditioned us
to crave exotic fruit contrary to the realms of your labor. Hell, we
even helped. Our men have bashed our women for sport, used you
for scapegoats to get in good with rednecks in white coats. Traitors
to our own cause. I was one before. A hypocrite. To taunt you in
front of peers, but catch the bus home to run up those stairs and
kiss my Black grandmother with the very lips I spat on you with.
How we've made a deity of Emily and a jest of Ebony. When jungle
fever has become the new black, what happens to the rest of the
rain forest?

How did America's piñata become its first lady? I'm learning. Even
the times when it felt like people looked right past you or saw only a
fraction of who you really are, you've always been young, gifted

10

and black. You proclaimed it. It manifested within you. You have a love affair with fire because that which gives light, must also endure burning. You've been phenomenal before Maya. Broadway since Lorraine. There's a resiliency about you. In a world that refuses to acknowledge that it sees color or race, you see the silver lining. It's as if a steel rod runs right through your head to your feet. You must be dipped in titanium, bronzed in elegance, enameled with grace and toasted with everlasting beauty. You can be the steam in our coffee or the buzz in our favorite drink. You can be anything to the man who deserves to taste you. You might not be everyone's cup of tea, but you're my shot of bourbon.

2 | Fruit of the Gods

You are made of brown sugar, cocoa, honey, gold and the strength of 1000 moons. You were sun kissed. Handpicked. The stork didn't have the grit to deliver you so you flew in on the wings of a sphinx. You are the mother of civilization. Nature modeled her ability to adapt to her surroundings after you. You are Destiny's child. Don't let anyone ever tell you different.

I formally renounce my light-skin privilege. The times I've been fair skinned enough to get away with a warning instead of ending up with my name on a t-shirt. The legs I've operated like heavy machinery because my golden tone is a quality that atones for whatever unfavorable characteristics I possess. I've watched from entitlement as you fight for a seat at the head of the table.

The black woman is the most unprotected, unloved woman on earth. She is the only flower on earth that grows unwatered. You would find more solace walking on the rings of Saturn than on the sidewalk. What did you do for America to alienate you so? There's a reason Black babies are on clearance in adoption agencies… why white babies are charged four times as much to espouse. How did you go from 3/5's a real person to 1/4th in retail value?

You are the spitting image of the motherland herself, before European exploration. You represent the earliest and longest lasting civilizations. You are the mecca of life itself. It's no coincidence Africa is the heart-shaped continent of the globe. That very organ of our home was confiscated from your bosom to build every star in that flag we pledge allegiance to. You are a painful reminder of our nation's shame.

That's why we idolize light-skin babies... why mixed kids are the "Future of America." If we blend it out, all the problems of the past will be absolved, but your beautiful deep melanin is worth preserving. Your fresh face with big regarding eyes, gorgeous, thick afro pulled back into a huge poof, with dark mahogany skin that glows like polished wood should not be allowed to fade out.

Your stamen produces pollen. Your seeds furnish kings. Your heart sows vitality. How many brutal centuries was your lineage able to withstand? How many family units did your predecessors keep afloat? From the day we arrived in cargo ships to the wars they shipped our sons back overseas. We need an extra day of the week, another hour on the clock, an additional holiday to show you how stupendous you are.

You are the standard of beauty. Cultures artificially enhance themselves to replicate your image. You are a reflection of GOD. So when I observe men abusing you, I understand it's an atheist trait to have nothing to die for. What a blessing it is to stand on the same planet as you. It was you who first put pen to papyrus so I don't mind acquiring carpal tunnel that travels from my forearm to my palm if the landscape of my art helps you globe trot.

Because it's about time we slay for our women. Time to pray for our women. Be true to our women. You've been a victim of circumstance for too long. It's time to be a victim of love. Your childhood is something you shouldn't have to recover from. You mature from pain, not age; and since you'll only be a toddler once, you deserve devotion. So daily, you should be clothed in Christ before you aspire to be another devil that wears Prada.

Bitch bad. Women good. Lady better. You didn't crawl out the baby carriage to sleep with all fours up in a doghouse. Your mental health is in jeopardy because Corporate America has created a cash cow by milking the clock. Queens spending their prime watching primetime, learning self-hate from love and hip-hop. Worse examples of matrimony in 1 episode on real housewives. Whether or not parental consent is given, media has a way of helping impressionable minds understand the Internet better than their parents.

You are not average. So allow me to be something acquiescent too. Society would rather have you be malevolent, waiting for handouts, scratching lottery tickets to use you as scapegoats but while you're still malleable, I find myself convicted to herd you in the direction of 401k plans instead of planned parenthood. I feel obligated to walk in and make sure before you walk out of the house, you know how your ebony is Greek for 'fruit of the gods', dense enough to sink in water but when polished, a wooden wand full of magical powers.

You are powerful enough to ward off the evil of this universe. Beautifully sheen with limited effort. Free of synthetics. Flawless before filters. Surrounded by sand paper. Years spent under the bus, now in the future facing extinction. You are modest and arrogant at the same time. Your mind is deeper than the Nile and skin stronger than an elephant's tusk.

A plot thickened.
A complicated combination.
And I want an entire village of you.

3 | A Do-Nothing Bitch

Does nothing for me.

How you swirl the brush over your face to blend your makeup doesn't intrigue me nearly as much as the skill it requires to accentuate the positive to bring out the best in people.

The measurements of your body better not be the only numbers you brag about. If so, the probability you plus me could ever equal better math is as likely as using a scientific calculator to solve my word problems.

'Cause a little black dress won't fetch you nearly as much success as a little bit of determination. Enamored by your entrepreneurial tendencies. Love how you built a firm foundation with all the bricks others threw at you.

I hope your favorite position isn't in the bedroom but CEO, because can't no pony you ride in the bedroom compare to how good you look jocking for a position. Beating those odds like the true thoroughbred you are.

Triple Crown. How you stand out in a room full of suits. Don't worry about coming home to a kitchen to prepare dinner. I've been taking some culinary classes because you deserve to be pampered the way you make me proud to call you "baby."

I'm not emasculated by your ambition. I'm empowered. I know your dating pool has gotten more shallow the deeper you've gotten into your career. Too many guys have a hard time playing second fiddle. They'd rather sow their royal oats than watch the Queen conquer. You're too good to settle for first lady. I wonder if boys would've given you a head start during gym class if they knew you'd have what it takes to be Head of State.

Love to see you ascend toward goals. Separating glass from ceiling. Moving mountains with your mind. Steadfast in your expectations. Steady in your formula. How many q-tips do you use to wipe out the words of doubters that attach to wax? Even dust has a hard time sticking to your shoulder the way you maneuver past every obstacle in your way.

I know your kinfolk is pressing you for a husband and some, kids but the trajectory you're on to accomplish is becoming folklore to the people of your hometown. I know you're not the type to put all your eggs in one basket, but your eggs are looking just as fertilized as the chicks who are trying to trap the men fighting with you for shares and stocks.

Thoughts of you come in waves, but tonight I'm drowning. Such a blessing whenever you share free time and tall tales with me. I show you undivided attention because I wholeheartedly relate to walking in the dark. The plight of a first generation scholar. How many brick walls did you push down to get where you are? How many friends fell by the wayside because they saw you doing better than them?

I wonder how many do-nothing bitches have choked on all the shit they talked about you? How many exes are keeping tabs on your endeavors so when you fall, they can spring forward with that "How you been stranger?" text? Choosy about who you surround yourself with because you are the company you keep and you can't afford to associate with anyone you need to push. You're too busy being pulled by your own vision.

Even if you never receive the humanitarian award for what you do in this world, we can share my Pulitzer Prize after I write your biography. You deserve voluntary body massages and butt rubs for how you work your ass off with your back against the wall. You're so well plugged. Just to be around you makes the hair on my skin rise because everything you touch leaves an electric shock.

Olivia Pope sized wine glasses filled to the brim to reward you for every scandal you've avoided. How you've seen brilliance without a compliment or a mirror. Sweating nothing, even with a fever. You've never had to rely on potential because you've got enough kilowatts to power your dreams, while your haters couldn't even find their own in the day with a flashlight. Marco Polo. It's blinding following you wherever your aspirations lead you.

What you do with the same 24 hours as the rest of us defies time. Intentional in everything you put your name to. Impeccable with every stroke of your genius. Birdseye view as I watch you wrap your talons around everything you embark on. Good footing for any branch of government. How you make it fly to be so politically correct. Watching your takeover with anticipation. Thank you for being better than average. And helping me be too.

4 | You Cute But Are You Down With The Revolution?

We can get ice cream together, listen to music, and travel galaxies. Go from puppy love to full grown to all dogs go to heaven. Shell out dollars at Disneyland, tailgate at the World Cup, pose in front of the Eiffel, but before I fall, are you down for the revolution?

No, you cannot plead the fifth. Not now, not here, not ever. I need to know if you can hold your head as high as your 6-inch heels 'cause if you can, you're worth the 7 stages of grief and I wouldn't mind decorating 8×10 frames across every inch of our home in your honor. Working 9 to 5's plus overtime to keep the lights on and candles lit just to keep you warmer. Staying at 10% body fat to keep your sexual appetite fulfilled. I have to know.

Because I will travel another 40 acres and a mule to find someone who's down. Do you still dig me in my dashiki? Or is my 3-button double breast the only thing that gets you leaking? If I grow locs, would you oil them with the same love you brush my deep waves with? Or would I be too afrocentric? At least that's what your friends say.

Do you have any hobbies that don't involve me? You want a white picket fence? But can you join me on the picket line to demonstrate against matters that cannot be waived or waited for anymore? Confederate flags waving as black churches are burning or do you not wanna get involved because you like living in the 60s more?

Did they make you hate your culture and love theirs instead? Should I apologize for my meltdowns and keep my rants to a minimum every time I see a man of color lying face down, explaining to us "it's not about race" now? If I kept up more with the Kardashians, watched Love & Hip Hop avidly just to reaffirm how much we allow exploitation and accept misogyny; obsessed over musical artists who have the platform to do so much but like so many leaders we needed, say so little, when it came time to their tour and I didn't buy a ticket, would you still be mad at me?

Politically speaking, are you used to being the one that got away? Are you socially awkward? Does the thrill of thousands of followers on social media keep you amused? Are you well behaved? Because those kind of women seldom make history now a days. Do you aspire to be a boss bitch, a trap queen, or just anything that mainstream sets as your glass ceiling? I want you to love me like Nelson. I want you to love me like Martin. I want you to love me like Lennon. I'm just trying to free you from being a slave to your mind. You are very welcome.

Are you in this for the making of more melanin cubs? You want the ceremonious wedding? The ring with more carats than vows? Or are you "'til death do us part" like our grandparents were? I'll boycott for a woman like Coretta Scott. Wait on death row for the next Maya Angelou. Take my train of thought off the tracks for a Rosa Parks.

I need to confess to you, I'm not as strong you think. My lips tremble when confronted by law enforcement, my chin drops when I see skinheads and my heart yearns for consolation when I listen to hip-hop on the radio. I don't wanna be hunted. I don't want to be a statistic. I don't want to be next but I can't help but feel there's a market for niggas and I'm on the selling block. Red. Black. Green. Garvey. Marley. Selassie. If you know what I mean.

What I'm looking for isn't a shirt I pull over my head to see if it fits. You don't have to be poetry in a world still learning the alphabet. I'm old enough to learn that sex ain't gon' keep you, so as my equal, I will treat you. I don't need you to be conflicted (although I've been the same). So when I get on my knee, don't say "I do." Say, "I'm down," for the revolution.

5 | Question Mark

Round of applause to the women who refuse to accept Professional Instagram Model as a career. The world is a much better place because of you. With summer coming to an end, the majority of these harlots are going to need to purchase a personality soon.
If you log onto Craigslist, you might be in luck, but if you logged into my IG and went in my recently liked photos, you'd discover a constellation of scantily clad strangers I haven't even been properly introduced to. But I wish somebody would call me thirsty…

I'm not a Looney Tunes character, but I've learned the hard way for a Wile E now. I lack the tunnel vision, or perhaps the speed the roadrunner possessed, to leave anyone thirsty for my attention in my dust. Didn't fall victim to any complex contraptions from acme products but these animal instincts have me right in line. Double tappin'. Do you ladies pop a cork for every time you catch us in your thirst trap?

With all the rows of duck lips in your profile, you should've added birdbrain to your bio. You failed to include #NudistColony to the dozens of hash tags you take into consideration during the 45 minutes of deliberation, which comes with posting. You would be the type to keep your account private when we all know it's public goods.

My spirit is willing, but when my flesh gets weak, robust trollops take over my timeline. "Ladies of the Night," my grandma would call them. Keeping my index scrolling and before you know it my blood pressure isn't the only thing rising. It's like you know how to train a dragon.

I've never taken a liking to slut shaming, but you can tell how many ladies settle for being tourist resorts rather than private islands based off the lack of self-esteem they demonstrate by throwing out flesh like bait to fish for compliments?

It seems like every 60 seconds, there's an image uploaded of someone with more hash tags than garments, ready to throw away the last teaspoon of nobility. But when you use that "single forever because men don't know how to court a woman" line, I'm minding my own business, sipping on my tea.

Holding onto notoriety, however, when the likes don't add up, you delete snapshots like they never existed but that's just a snip it of the hard work you go through to be renowned. It must tickle ya fancy when people call you by your username when you're waiting outside at the club when it's free before 9.

I wonder how many arguments would be null and void, if I could push the candles you so perfectly configured around the ring of the tub in that dark lagoon before you said "cheese" and went spread eagle all over the faucet.

How many breakups could be prevented if that brand new necklace turned your neck green before you took a selfie and we saw how awesome your boobs looked, stampeding out of your crop top into our smartphone.

I encourage your gym flow, but what if you got a charley horse from doing all the fake squats in your boy shorts without a weight rack in sight. You must mistake us all for dumb broads because I know you don't have any calluses under those work out gloves because you've never picked up a dumbbell.

Racking up your thousands of followers, but losing whatever makes you one in a million isn't the trade I hope you're aiming for. In the same breath it takes for me to brag to my friends about how phenomenal you are, they probably finished masturbating in their tube sock.

Not that you care, but does it matter that nobody even knows what color your eyes are because they're so preoccupied with every other body part? Tomb Raider. Exploring the dead ends of your carcass that leave nothing to our imagination. Your body may be built like a Benz, but your temple is in ruins.

I know if I strip down to my Tommy Hilfiger, I figure I'll draw a cougar out of the herd. And I'm fully aware that these college loans have clustered together and they have no intentions of just paying themselves. Although, if you're stimulated enough you might manage to pull a Tyga out of your hat.

Don't complain about attracting the same type of guy when you lack anything worth desiring once they cum to their senses. A woman who is a riddle, wrapped inside of an enigma, doesn't seek attention because they're always under surveillance. The mystery alone is worth a curiosity trip. And what's better to return to than a question mark?

6 | Dear White People,

I know Halloween is around the corner and you're looking forward to beer pong, keg stands and party hopping in Santa Barbara, but I want to let you know what the truly scary thing is...you can't tell the difference between a costume and cultural appropriation. We cannot be "hombres" if you think rocking a sombrero to a party is something I can just sweep under the rug. Just because there's a bounty for every illegal immigrant, you're not required to kick an entire race when they're already down.
Ponchos with hysterical black mustaches might show you have a sense of humor but I can show you pictures of Border Patrol detaining undocumented immigrants that match that same description. Using a group of people for target practice to protect the imaginary fence of a country they helped build from the ground up.

Modeling a tequila shooter outfit to enhance a Latin American look explains how out of touch you are with the rest of the world. Tell me how many stars you see while donning an illegal alien jail costume after you get knocked into the next world.

I can't see myself kicking it with anyone sporting a jumbo afro wig because they wanna be Afrocentric one day of the year, but benefit from privilege the other 364. Wearing locs that you consider dreadful and making light of their nature doesn't give you a free pass to pose with them for Instagram.

Painting on black faces is an act punishable by catching a black eye. Just because you saw Straight Outta Compton in theaters doesn't warrant you to be a Black thug; unless you want to be personally dropkicked back to the suburb you came out of.

If you think you can get away with saying the N-word, please take note... I hope you have family to warn you before you walk out of the house in your Aunt Jemima or Uncle Tom attire. Knocking on a door in slave get-up, I hope you master your fear of heights 'cause you might get dropped like a bad habit.

Putting on camouflage and rocking bullets around your neck might be a great Taliban impression, but if you ain't the man that can handle heat in the kitchen I would reconsider unless you have an appetite for disaster. Acting like we haven't labeled every person wearing a turban a "terrorist" can't be too far removed from distant memory. Especially with the anniversary of 9/11.

You might not be told to kick rocks in your sexy Arab attire at a party, but women have been stoned to death for revealing too much skin. Don't be the straw that breaks the camel's back. A sexy harem belly dancer could get a pass if you were Middle Eastern, but since you're not, don't. It would serve you right to have the taste slapped out of your mouth for such tasteless acts. A bolly ho outfit might be innocent enough, but that should speak to your inability to think again.

Just because being a Geisha is beautiful, doesn't mean you should paint your face white and imitate one. Especially if you actually dress like a teenage victim of sexual trafficking giving happy endings in the most crummy massage parlor in San Bernardino.

Pretending to be a mismatch pan-asian doll is a bad idea no matter how amazing the bun on the top of your head is. Chinaman wardrobe isn't funny in any setting. Especially when you don't know how offensive that term is.

Looking like a sexy Chinese Take-Out Maid might be on your small list of goals for the year, but I would pray you don't walk down the wrong part of Chinatown. Wearing a mask that emphasizes small eyes isn't even worthy of a conversation unless we're talking non-verbal.

Finding a balance between being edgy and racist has become a national pastime for too many Americans this time of the year. Mocking an entire group of people with diverse phenotypic traits or ethnic backgrounds might win you best costume award, but it'll lose you my friendship...for whatever that's worth.

Think twice before you get that costume off the rack at Spirit. Party City has good deals, but don't pay for it later. I love Spencer's like anyone else, but let me be frank with you when I say, you might actually have to wear extra makeup to work the next day. Not an advocate for violence but I have no patience for ignorance. Racial bigotry runs through this country like an electric current. You wear that costume for one night. I wear that stigma for life.

Thanks,

Management

7 | Kryptonite

I'm nothing more than a muse. My chocolate satisfies that sweet tooth. I am your backstage pass to our culture. I am not prince charming. I am your rose that grew from concrete that you rub in the face of your subordinates and strangers who pass us in public. You can't seem to wrap your head around the concept of me tying my hair with a du-rag, yet when my waves are on display; you don't press me. Your parents can barely hold eye contact with me, but since I have a college degree they clench onto my every word. The negative images of us feed your desire to find someone exactly like me.

I attract a wide range of women who aren't Black. I fit into their "type." They always make it a point to indicate "You're not like other Black men," as if I should feel grateful that out of all the stray dogs at the pound, they found me as the most compatible companion.

I am who they choose to live their fantasy out with. They admire how I don't let my race handicap me from my hobbies deemed "non-black." I rock jump. I sky dive. I snowboard. I jump in the pool. The dare devil in me stirs the curiosity in them.

They love that I'm a Republican, that I'm open to dating outside of my race, and that I say the n-word in their company, which they take as permission to assimilate into "my nigga." I am nothing more than an anomaly.

They don't know much about Black fraternities, but they love to attend our parties. They can twerk to any current rap song on the radio, but don't know the original artists the songs were sampled from. Their favorite athlete is Black, but they don't even watch the sport they play in.

They admire that I'm an activist and I support #BlackLivesMatter, but when I ask them to join in on a nonviolent march, they've got other plans. They submit to me in the bedroom and compare the size of my dick to other men, as if that's the way to stroke my ego. They discuss how beautiful our kids will look because they'll be "mixed," as if it would disappoint them if the baby ever came out with dark pigmentation and unyielding hair texture, as if a baby born without colored eyes is an abomination.

A woman I showed interest in, once asked me to help her daughter become more confident in her "Blackness." Show her child how to be proud that she stands out in a primarily white school because as someone who never grew up with certain "Black problems," I would give her daughter better advice than herself personally.

As if my skin tone held the key to unlocking self-esteem. The way I carry myself exhibits charm and charisma; therefore, since you found my assertiveness attractive I could rub off on your child? All because I don't walk with my head bowed down like society expects. Because I don't respond to "boy" when a police officer address me as one. Because I am dominant behind closed doors and know how to lift your legs behind your head like I'm operating a forklift while I'm power drilling. Because I check you when you speak to me in a condescending manner; so you understand I'm not the one.

I can't be your kryptonite. I will not settle for your weakness when I am the ability to be someone's strength. I will not garner an interracial relationship because of the "cool factor." I will not be your arm accessory because this kind of black looks good on any red carpet.

I can't be your forbidden fruit. Just because you wanted to live a disobedient life to stick it to your father, I will not play accomplice. I won't be your "grass is greener on the other side" either because my Blackness comes with its own set of difficulties I keep below the surface that I'm still coping with almost 3 decades later.

No matter how many rap lyrics of Ludacris you can recite, if you aren't able to roll out of bed with me and see a work in progress instead of a prize on a mantle then move, bitch. Get out the way.

I am not your personal urban dictionary for ebonics. I don't like Tyler Perry movies so don't bring over *Madea Goes to Jail*. I've never played dominoes so at BBQ's don't ask me to go with the guys. I don't want you to be submissive because that's what you think I like.

33

If you like your men like your coffee only, let me excuse myself. I like my women sapiosexual with a dark side and so inattentive to the complexion of my skin that they're completely absorbed by all the vibes I emit.

I want to be viewed as so out of this world when people ask us where we met the memory of the coffee shop where we first made contact makes you see stars. And no matter how distant that was you easily confuse it for the Milky Way. You better not fetishize my culture if you ever want to see a future with me.

What you're mixed with is the smallest ingredient to the recipe we are to create together.

8 | Assholes Anonymous

That fresh batch of bird shit that landed on your windshield when you drove outta the car wash isn't coincidence, it's calculated. There's a reason why that soda you were craving on ya lunch break outta the vending machine exploded like a hand grenade soon as you pulled the tab on it. You're the kinda person who awkwardly walks in without knocking before I can finish masturbating. You must have been conceived through anal sex because you're an asshole. And not like that "say goodnight to the bad guy, Al Pacino and say hello to my little friend" kinda way, but in that open a box of pistachio and white chocolate macaroons after 40 days of lent and finding a dead fly in the middle. You wear it like a badge of honor, but it fits more like a tail on a donkey. You're the guy after gym class in locker rooms who takes cologne baths in Axe, thinking of attracting pheromones. Smoking vape pens on the table next to me while I'm on my first date at a "make your reservation weeks in advance, take ya girl to feel like a woman" restaurant.

You're that self-described asshole. The one who writes it in your bio, who sends direct messages to people that don't accept your friend request because you have not an ounce of dignity. You screenshot conversations of people caught up, basking in your admiration, then straight up post them because you weren't

35

satisfied enough as a kid pouring salt on slugs. You graduated to pouring salt on wounds. You were the kind of child who pulled wings off of ladybugs. You're despicable. Your soul must be compiled of the same tar pits that scientists discovered fossils in. Poetic justice would be if you came back in your next lifetime as a urinal.

You're the reason why pride has taken more young lives than suicide. Why we walk around like empty drones until we have enough shots of Patron to make drunk dials because after we drown our blood stream, real feelings surface. You're responsible for the deep wave of hipsters, who in this new age of self-preservation, profess they can't find a fuck to give. Orphans to their emotions. Introverted, but loudest one in the chat rooms. No social skills visible but online, social life poppin'. Worried about being popular, living between hash tags, off ya parents' comforter.

You're a poser. If your mother knew she would've given birth to someone that addressed themselves as an asshole after she spent most of the year pregnant, those painful hours in labor and even more time on a name you'd answered to, she would've just swallowed you, instead. Been in the company of people like you in several forms. Nothing more unattractive than when the opposite sex lists that as a redeeming quality. That don't impress me much but I'm flushed you're interested. Makes sense why you got diarrhea of the mouth. However, someone clearly skipped the memo "you are the company you keep," so what do I look like standing in a pile of feces?

You don't give a shit because you're emotionally constipated. You care, but you ain't got the balls to admit it. You might've used that facade to make a young freshman hand over her v-card because she was naive, but try that gimmick on a Queen who you can't weasel over beer pong; where mental stimulation isn't foreplay, it's a prerequisite. You're under the impression that the more inaccessible you are, the more attractive you appear. You're overcompensating for something. You probably ask, "Did you cum?" Explains why you never get second servings.

It's like a viral strain how people keep claiming they're assholes only because the last one rubbed off on them. It's nothing more than a chain message and you're square enough to be apart of the pyramid scheme. I know y'all meet once a week behind closed doors to confess how tired you are of being fraud. Hope you don't try too hard to clog ya arteries of how you feel so that if you ever have a heart attack and doctors try to operate, they can't find yours anymore. You're not an asshole by nature, you strive for that title. The jig is up. Put down that Marshall Mathers LP. Go cop that Take Care. You can thank me later.

9 | Homophobia is Gay

Newsflash: You can still love your man and be manly, but you would think that's a taboo in the black community where masculinity plays such a pivotal role in how we chose our friends. Recently, I was tagged in photographs in West Hollywood and within hours, I had people texting me asking if I still liked women. Like being around my friends who were homosexual would affect my sexual preference or seduce me into changing preferences like I do pajamas. One friend asked, "Are you comfortable in your own skin?" Well I could trim up around my waist, add some muscle to my legs and even turn the hands of time back so my hairline wouldn't be so thin in the front, but when it comes to being around people who are different than me, I couldn't be more comfortable. In fact, maybe I'm too comfortable. I'm too tired after my 9-5 to work another shift living a double life.

Maybe my most redeeming quality is that I treat people how I want to be treated. Above all the lessons my grandmother taught me, that was my favorite. So many gays are made to feel worthless by cruel and relentless people. I chose a long time ago I would leave people better than how I found them. One of my friends interviewed me the other day for his magazine. "How does it feel to be heterosexual with such a strong connection to the LGBT community?" My answer: "An honor."

It's been such a stigma that birds of a feather flock together so if I surround myself with one group of people, I must be like them too. But my company always varies. I spend my time with atheists, does that mean I don't believe in GOD? I hang around people without college degrees. Does that make mine obsolete? I have friends who are deaf. Does that impair my hearing? I like to be around white people, does that make me less black? I even associate with strippers. Does that mean you're gonna see me sliding down a pole at Spearmint Rhino?

It just so happens, I love being around my gay friends because they know how to have fun and I don't feel like I need to apologize for my mannerisms. I can sing lyrics to Lady Gaga and not worry about what they think of me. I can wear a floral top and not have to explain why I chose that. The simple fact that I can be myself unapologetically is something we all yearn for. It just so happens with one group of people it comes that much more naturally.

I remember crying in the arms of my best friend once, as he held me in college. Didn't have to ask him to keep it a secret. I recall having sleepovers and letting my guy friends come over, as we played video games all night. Wasn't worried about what kids said on the playground. You think now if I go to a gay bar and dance my ass off, I'm worried about what someone will think on Facebook?

39

Being gay is not a crime. I, personally, don't believe it's a sin. I won't use GOD to justify prejudice. You wouldn't believe how many women I've met, who upon getting to know me, confess, "I always thought you were gay." Maybe it was my colored contacts or how I use to get my eyebrows threaded. Probably even when I was Prince for Halloween a few years back. Or maybe because most of the good men these days are gay, you were under the impression I batted for the other team too? How happy they are when they learn how I swing.

I wish I could tell you how liberating it is to choose your friends based off what you have in common, instead of what public perception is. I wouldn't be surprised if all my groomsmen were homosexual down the line. Would that make my wedding less traditional? I have one in particular that will probably be my children's godfather. Am I worried about my son's impressionable mind? Absolutely not. You clearly must not have any idea who the father is. I will not be pigeonholed by members of society. Caged without the ability to be free without labels.

I can go anywhere with anyone and be completely comfortable. I had dinner tonight with one of my best friends who couldn't keep his eyes off the male server. Did that make my time at cheesecake factory any less enjoyable? On the contrary, that much more. To know me is to love me. To question me because you don't know yourself is a completely different story for a completely different time. You're not scared to be around people who are different; you're just an asshole. And love always wins. Homophobia is gay.

10 | Graveyard Shift

You didn't need a good sense of direction to find the Do Not Disturb sign hung on the doorknob. You're the disobedient type. Record of insubordinate behavior as long as your butt-length hair. You close your fist and raise your lathered, cocoa-buttered knuckles to pound, but feeling Troublesome, you stop.

Instead you grip the knob of the door and twist, wearing nothing but a trench coat and a mischievous smirk across your face. You cross the threshold. Now there is no turning back. Not quite breaking and entering, but since you're naughty by nature this will have to suffice. For now.

Christian Louboutin, peep toe, platform pumps lead you into the dimly lit room. Your high heels tapping the hard wood resemble a drum roll. Soon, you will sound like a siren. You follow the aroma of freshly burned incense. They lead to me. Your silhouette has already set the mood so before this evening's chain of events; I've already telepathically undressed you.

Quite the religious ceremony indeed. You walk tentatively forward like it's Altar Call. Extending my palm to meet yours, I place a moist kiss on the back of your hand. I watch the hairs on it rise. My untamed beard fondles your freshly manicured set of nude nails as I take my paws off.

Purposely leaving a trail of Dolce & Gabbana cologne to kick-start your pheromones. Foreplay began as soon as you came in and it will last until you're begging me to be inside you. You have a long string of being disappointed, but tonight I hope you're ready for the unusual.

I pour you a glass of Hennessy on the rocks. No need to debate if it's 1/2 half empty or not because the moon is full. Tension so thick you can cut it with a knife, but each second waiting gives you a spoonful of ideas and if done right, your taste buds will find it irregular to crave fast food again. Enjoy this smorgasbord.

I've already told you what I want to do to you in great detail. Anticipation makes pleasure more intense, so don't worry, everything is going to be amazing. I provide a rather exhilarating deep tissue massage, free of charge, to help you ease your mind. Releasing that chronic muscle tension because I would hate for you to pull anything.

I take a detour to your buttocks, which starts your engine. You want me right now. Not a minute later. You grab my red, satin, bow tie and tow me to the headboard. I follow your lead. You unbutton my Armani, striped, slim fit, two-button suit as my fingers run wild through your pasture of hair, yanking handfuls at a time.

No weapon formed against you shall prosper, but this powerful tool of seduction forces you to bite your bottom lip. You can see my dick print so vividly through my pants that you mistake it for an eggplant. Regardless, you came for ripe produce so you can't wait to bag it. You disconnect my buckle and slide my belt off. Unbothered knowing that you are going to be another notch on them.

You lift your leg from the carpet to the ceiling letting it rest on my shoulder. With flexibility like that in your arsenal I can only imagine what other equipment you have stored for me. I use my teeth to take off your heel letting it drop like a nuke. You sink 6 inches. **No one man should have all this power.** Leaning like the Tower of Pisa I lift you up and remove the other. Your fingers running down my deep waves as you return to gravity. Clearly you're not afraid of heights.

You're here for a good time, not a long time, so I'm aware of the unspoken non-disclosure agreement. You rip off my shirt, but remove my french cuff links with care. I'm standing in my Calvin Klein boxer briefs as you lick your lips but I'm no midnight snack. Today I'm open for business 24 hours; I hope you brought an appetite for this graveyard shift.

You push me on the bed then untie your trench coat. My mouth drops to the floor. Nothing but lace. You put your hair into a ponytail, which tells me it's time to back up all that talk. Our mouths meet like we raced out of the starting gate. Hard. Messy. Passionately. Surprised we didn't sprain a box spring.

My tongue slithers up the side of your neck as I bite down into your collard greens, nipping at your tenderloin. You let out a moan. Loud enough to think you've been holding onto it all day; it would startle even the heaviest sleeper. I have a foot fetish so excuse my curiosity if I want to see if you can arch your back like your heel.

Your pedicure didn't go unnoticed and your sterling silver toe ring set off my magnetic field. I suckle your breast, one at a time. You breathe heavily into my ear lobe, fogging my judgment. Tapping into unused resources. Saliva hanging off your nipple piercings. I make it my mission to leave hickies in places nobody will ever find.

Slapping your ass until I see handprints. Came on an empty stomach so don't think you're getting out of this with all those groceries. Intoxicated by your demeanor, I know you like it rough, so although I will handle with care you won't be leaving in the same condition you arrived. Testing to see if you still adore me with my hands around your neck.

I came to devour you in all places making 50 Shades of Grey look like child's play. This isn't beginners luck. I pull your edible undies to the side making a mental note to save room for dessert, parting the sheets like Holy water, tossing pillows to the floor, using them like knee pads because with a Brazilian wax like that I might as well thank GOD.

You open your legs. Spread Eagle. Access granted. Eyes covered with bondage to prevent peaking. My idea of a blind date. Wrists cuffed above your head. If you're late for work in the morning tell your boss you got tied up with something. Your thick luscious garden of Eve greets me. I forgot flowers so I plant my chin into your soil.

I suck your outer lips then trace my initials into the inner realms. You're dripping with desire, so I catch your juices with my goatee. Treat my facial hair like your body towel. The focal part of your thigh is tender so I taste it. Nuzzling my face into your crotch, I separate the lips and run my tongue up and down the layers of your flesh.

I tongue fuck you, but slow my momentum as I approach with caution over your tiny pearl heading into Heaven's gate. As I work the tip of your iceberg I begin to feel you tremble. I latch onto your clit as you start to come down from your orgasm. Free falling. Rhythmic contractions in your lower abdomen. Followed by spastic hip movements.

You tell me you're coming so I give you a hand. Fingering your g-spot as you start squirting. I take my time signaling, acknowledging your caution signs. Stroking your body, caressing your breasts. Leaving my finishing touches. Room service is bound to think this floor re-installed waterbeds.

You hold the sheets for dear life but it's too late. You're discombobulated. Lips quivering. Both sets. La petite mort. French for 'mini death.' I don't need to go out on a limb to know you climaxed. You would think I read a pussy licking guide the way the ink dried and pages turned to dust. Bibliophile.

ASSERTIVE

11 | Mr. Potato Head

I wanna stop seeing my psychiatrist. I've gotten to know each of the disorders I'm suffering from quite personally and you could say we all mutually decided it would be best to cohabitate. They rent out separate lobes so if I ever come off the dome please forgive me. My writing has picked up a full head of steam so apparently there are benefits of having a loco motive. Sure I talk to myself, but sometimes I need expert advice. I've been so emotionally disturbed lately, I took a personality test to see if I was the type of person I'd want to be with.

I used to wear makeup to cover up my acne scars. Puberty left my face a bumpy road so to smooth things out I laid a liquid foundation. Before the sun rose I tiptoed to empty bathroom stalls when I lived in my dormitory to apply my ugly secret. Lived a heterosexual lifestyle, but was called every gay slur in the book. I must've grown an extra layer of skin that year because even though I was bullied so much I almost dropped out, the only company I managed to keep was the dean's list. I would blatantly lie even though reality made it so that brutally honest people hated what they didn't understand. I had to cope with puberty's side effects along with my general education core curriculum requirements. I could fill a flash drive with all the feats I didn't go for because I was insecure. Prayed for the day my skin oil wasn't the chink in my armor so when those rough patches cleared up, I had some steam to blow.

The juxtaposition of growing up mixed, being fetishized for certain black qualities yet hating blackness, that was me. My big nose kept me from ever sticking it in anyone's business, but it didn't prevent anyone from attacking mine. I was nicknamed Joe the Camel before I had smooth character. Must've went through a dozen databases before I realized I was the butt end of the joke. Never watched a day of SpongeBob, but I knew who Squidward was. At track practice, varsity players treated me like a hurdle. Almost resorted to Columbine tactics, but I had under armour before it was copy written. Used to look forward to October so I could cover my face with costumes just so I could look consensual. The way they treated me, my high school reunion was worth an appearance, but I didn't go because I was channeling all my time to prove people wrong that never mattered and 10 years later, if I returned for validation that would have been giving them the victory lap.

If I had a silver dollar for every time I was referred to as "DSL," I would've used that rainy day money to nip tuck that cloudy judgment. Dick-sucking lips was an acronym I knew first hand no matter the arms distance I tried to separate myself. Didn't feel comfortable in my own skin so to find common ground, I pursed my lips to hold them from anyone ready to snatch the smile off my face. Quite ironic when old friends say I'm brand new because I don't remember them breaking bread when I was an ugly ducking. To think I was so close to going under the knife due to all the people that made a daily visit of going below the belt. When I finally grew into my lips it must have been when the rest of the world started to finally see the beauty in them.

Call me crazy but there was a time I would have traded parts of myself into Hasbro for pushpins. Just so I could manipulate myself to my own liking. Mr. Potato Head how I put a smile on for people constantly trying to piece me together. No stranger to being misunderstood. Felt botched because I wasn't made for everyone. The only treatment plan that could nurse my imbalance was surgically removing the pieces of me that wanted to be liked by everyone else. Feel like a mad scientist the way my spine was stitched so strong back together you would think I attached mechanical appendages. Standing exposed without feeling repulsed. No longer the proverbial lamb to slaughter. Had to lose my marbles like a game of mancala. Addition by subtraction. Or maybe it's just physics, no wonder my alter egos collide.

12 | Nahla

You don't have to play doctor to know you have my heart. No stethoscope required to hear how loud it beats for you. Don't have to monitor my oxygen to know every time you say my name you steal my breath. You can hold the sperm sample vials too because despite the fact you never came from me, I still belong to you. My favorite girl. The day I signed for guardianship, we established that there was nothing you could say out of line for me to love you any less. Nothing black and white about our relationship. Would've signed that dotted line a million more times if it meant you could understand how signature you are to me and that this love was written in ink.

I remember when you were premature, how many nights you immediately daydreamed behind hospital walls, seconds after you came out of the womb. Did it wake you in the middle of your sleep to overhear all the conversations I had with GOD? We spent hours arguing about how important your life was in my prayers. Went back and forth to reach an understanding about how directly proportional you continuing your life was to mine.

After watching you fight so hard for life I decided I could never leave you in your corner without a coach. You southpaw. Leaving that little body in a ventilator, as we didn't know which breath would be your last. Nights passed while I weighed with my faith as it was left swinging on the pendulum. I attempted suicide days before you ever brought me new life. Butterfly effect. Broke out of my cocoon once you gave me a viable reason to believe I had wings.

I was a coward and when things got too heavy I didn't think I had the strength to see myself across the finishing line. I still hate myself for that moment to this day. Tried to swallow an entire bottle of my doctor's prescription pills while driving drunk to help me piece it together after my grandmother died. I don't think I've ever told anybody that.

There were so many people I encouraged to keep fighting while I was behind my own enemy lines. Used to think I was my best company, but I was ready to use friendly fire on myself. Sad to ever think suicide was an answer because I wasn't asking the right questions. GOD redirected me to the right ones.

And then you came, in all your glory. I remember when you came home how I thought I had met the most beautiful woman to date. Saw our resemblances because all your baby photos we took, you look like me.

Can't believe that first year of your life, babysitting. Friends asking how I used that college degree... I'm letting it sit on the wall while I raise a Queen. Remember each crawl. Each step. Each fall. Each cry out of the carriage. Each second you looked at me and I knew you said you loved me with your eyes.

You were full-time on my schedule. Nothing came before you. How much I relish that role. Who knew, even though you were artificially inseminated you could be loved by a human love no greater. You'll never know your father because as long as you grow, you'll never get the chance to see his name on any Google search.

He gave his sperm to science to make this world a greater place for women that couldn't get pregnant with a partner. So many days I was asked, "What is she to you?" "Why is she in all your pics?" "Is that your child?" No answer required.

She's mine and I am hers. They wanna know what's the source of inspiration for my writing? It's you. You're the reason behind every letter I type. Ain't a bone in anyone's body that could be stronger than the ones I use in my finger to write about you. How could a bond be tighter? How could anything be stronger? You are the reason I'm still alive and now everyone knows.

13 | One More Round

I loved you before I was legal. The taste of you lingered through my entire childhood. My grandfather introduced us at his bar. Whiskey was your name and on school days, you were the perfect nightcap. A few shots later, I'd stumble up the stairs. The scorching feeling in my stomach neutralized my burning curiosity. On the rare occasions my grandmother suspected your scent before she kissed me goodnight, I called you mouthwash.

I should hate you for what you did to the men in my family. My grandfather and father both sacrificed families to be with you. I knew how to handle you in moderation, although guilt caused an early separation. We weren't on good terms again until college. It tore at my conscience to look my Nana in the eye and lie like all the other men in my family; so I parted ways. But without parental supervision, we picked back up in my dorm room where we left off.

You were there for that middle passage from boy to man. When I struggled making friends and made the dean's list, who did I share the good news with? After those intramural debates I won, who did our coaches take us to celebrate with? Before I got on those stages to rock the mic, who took the cool off? You're the reason I got over my fear of flying. You were there when I lost my virginity. You were there when my girlfriend had that miscarriage. You watched me grow up.

But you also had front row seats when I self-destructed. When I got in trouble for domestic violence, officers smelled you all over me. That time I showed up to tutor after the pub; you're the reason I was fired. When we hung out with someone who wasn't 21 and they got alcohol poisoning who took the blame? After I blacked out at a tailgate and woke up in handcuffs, who was found drunk in public? You've made a fool of me. Constantly rolling my eyes as my grandmother rolled in her grave.

I should hate you but I can't let go because you make a great companion on Sunday mornings watching football and Thursday nights watching Scandal. You've given me courage. The type to pick up that phone and say what my heart's been screaming. The kind to approach someone that my body's been yearning for. And at those all-day parties in Vegas, you've made the most unattractive people somewhat appealing. I wouldn't be quite the karaoke singer without you and I doubt I'd have the moves on the dance floor.

But I'll never be able to condone the pain I've caused when I've gone over my limit. The emotional ache I've caused to the people who loved me most. Their only mistake was hanging on to my every word but like an untrained hang glider, I watched crash without a parachute. Catch 22. How you have brought the teddy bear out in me, as well as, the boogieman from under the bed. How good I've become at coloring my life with the chaos of trouble.

You'd think I had my last sip after all the great things I've let slip between my fingers all that time I spent clinging onto you. I used to think you were a coping mechanism, helping me adjust to a social life, but time has revealed you to be the bane of my existence. And lately, I've craved the sight of a blue moon. Even a shot of tequila would hit the spot. For brunch, how clutch would bottomless mimosas be?

It was never the pain or the hangover that made me question myself. It was always the question of whether or not I could still be 'myself' without 'you,' would I be able to make such killer first impressions without killing myself? Could people adore me without the alcohol? Did I have to be under the influence to take someone to cloud 9?

I'm not an alcoholic but I'd rather not feel inadequate anymore. You've been a bad habit since I was 8. That was 20 years ago. I am greater than what I have suffered through. I liked myself better before I met you. I miss my optimism. I miss my blind spots for people's bullshit. I miss my jovial spirit. And being an artist means forever healing your own wounds and at the same time endlessly exposing them. Forever writing responsibly.

14 | Phoenix

I'm sorry. For never believing I had shoulders broad enough to fit into that cape. Instead, I found a more fitting role as antagonist. I was never fully committed to you because you were only a half-blood. And since I despised your father and you always talked about mine, we were born enemies. Children of the grave, how much time we spent biting each other's heads and dismembering limbs because our family tree left us with splinters. We never found time to patch up those differences.

I was supposed to be the best friend you couldn't get rid of. Instead, I was the first of a revolving door of men who walked away without looking back. I don't recall sharing childhood memories or discussing grown up dreams. Just weekend custody visits where I returned back to my grandmother's, hoarse from shouting at the top of my lungs how your birth certificate should of been an apology from the condom factory.

I spent my adolescence ripping into you like you were my adversary. When schoolmates asked if I had a sister, I denied your existence. When Christmas came, I was the coal in your stocking. When boys teased you about your appearance, I was a bystander. I wanted nothing to do with you because you were a reminder of my mother's transgression. Felt like open season whenever you came into my peripheral. Quail hunting. You were an echo of what went wrong. A parrot in the oven. Apparently you joined the wrong flock. Threw off the formation and I couldn't let you off the hook, so your goose was cooked.

Years later, I see the effect of my insubordination. I broke your wings at home before you ever left the nest. As an adult, I see you struggling to put food on the table and it eats at me. I hear the sound of rejection in your voice even when I accept your calls. You have your head down even when I open up my arms. There's no richter scale to equal the damage caused by me turning your world upside down, but it had to have been amplified when your own parents abandoned you.

But here I am. Making up for lost time. Filling in the blanks. How we went from pen pals where you were in the armed forces to next of kin when I graduated college is a tale of two cities. I send your letters through mail and make phone calls because I'd like to think my cadence is something you can't hear in text and my cursive can make you feel as connected as my words are designed to be. Each time I offer you relationship advice, deep down I'm crossing my fingers because I intend on staying true to my pinky swear of becoming the world's best uncle alive.

Truth be told, I never would've sought out my fraternity if I fulfilled my mission statement as an older sibling. If I could take a time machine back to the playground I would punch out every boy that declared you had cooties. Instead of you waiting at the bus stop, I would of pulled up in my broke down hoopty to scoop you up and skip homework to check out matinee movies. And on prom night, I would've given that overprotective speech to your underage date with my brass knuckles, so he knew I meant business.

I see you reaching the end of your twenties with more questions than answers. I know I'm fashionably late; but thankfully, there is no time limit on finding your soul mate. When you apologize for rambling, you better understand there's nothing else more important I'd rather be doing than listening. When you complain about the things you don't like about yourself, I hope I have enough brotherly love to drown out your insecurities. I've been practicing walking in a straight line for years so I can make sure I don't need too many rehearsals to walk you down the aisle. I discovered so much inside of me that I'm finally following the clues of how to pour it all out. Thanks for your patience.

Look up in the sky. It's not a plane. It's not superman. It's a phoenix. Renewed. Reborn. Restored.

15 | Antique Shopping

Barring any unforeseen head injuries, consider my brain property of science research and education when I bite the dust. Always wanted to make a difference long after I'm gone and since I know Alzheimer's runs in my family, maybe when the smoke clears my granddaughter won't need letters in her pasta as a senior citizen to remember the alphabet.

Playing small does not serve the world. I am the universe in ecstatic motion and since I've been on this planet many times over I figure I've absorbed enough data to be the cure. Earth is only college to me and I've learned so many lessons backpacking through different eras with this linear thinking. I feel like a super senior taking freshman seminar.
No matter how many greys I collect on my head, I'm still evergreen. I like my breakfast at Tiffany's when I'm feeling 60's with a side order of Green Eggs and Ham, if it's just what the Dr. ordered.

Some Dorothy Dandridge if I want that old feeling back, but when I want a song of love that clings to me, Nat King Cole knows exactly what unforgettable words to say.

Been a prince of Egypt before I ever opened up the book of Exodus, I too, sang America long before I ever stood for the pledge of allegiance.

Had "Hercules" tatted on my forearm before I ever picked up a pen and since they say it is mightier than the sword, call it trite or narcissistic but like the legend, I'm writing lines that are likely to live for ages.

If you want to feel the world, hold hands with a writer. My generation is too lukewarm, so I'm out of touch. Although I was born in the 80's, maybe by the time I've kicked the bucket my case study will prove I gravitated toward old souls without a metal detector because I treasure antique spirits.

The latest media scandal doesn't kick start my motorcycle nearly as much as reclining at Barnes & Noble. I read *The Alchemist* in one sitting, but *To Kill A Mockingbird* is literature every adult should read before they die because the experience is the reward.

I have a tumultuous relationship with Mother Nature although she is a murderer; I've learned more from her personification than from the nature of humans who kill for more time just to spend it with people who wouldn't even take a bullet for them.

Lessons such as learning to dance in the rain, instead of waiting for the storm to pass, or enduring the uphill struggle by visualizing the view from the top, helps my anxiety take a hike whenever doubt creeps in. Keeping negative thoughts at bay because my ability to relax has been in direct proportion to my ability to trust life.

No wonder I had such a hard time fitting in; stars in my eyes and books in my hands. Socially strange on the playground, maladaptive daydreamer in the classroom, but around my grandparents' peers, no matter how random the topics got, I could hold a conversation down like I didn't need to come up for air.

Or maybe I learned to be grateful for every breath when I lost every strand of my curly hair before the tooth fairy got a chance to reimburse me for baby teeth. When I was twisting prescription bottles to survive prior to ever tasting a Flintstone vitamin.

I remember laying bedside, reading cards from classmates, waking up to meals before dawn, feeling like an inmate, pain in my joints before I ever became a pain in the ass. Wondering if Kawasaki would put a nail in my coffin before my first crush got a chance to pin a corsage on my tuxedo.

Walking out of chemo with powers beyond the physical. Just a spiritual being overcoming another human experience and since then, it's as if everything is a miracle.

My soul is a mix tape, but no one owns a cassette player anymore. You might be a great outlet, but can I entrust you with my aux cord? I'm a compilation of many songs.

I can let you try my Wu Tang style, if you're able to strum my pain with ya fingers. Perhaps I can be the blues in your left thigh. Or the funk in your right.

16 | Gift Wrapped

I had a dream that I woke up in Texas with a wedding ring on. But that wasn't real. Unless we're talking about when my mother didn't understand the concept of visitation rights after she lost custody of me, so she kidnapped me and took me to San Antonio for a year without uttering a peep. I remember as a kid having to hide under bunk beds or in car trucks when my grandma hired detectives to come find me. So forgive me if I ever enjoy the thrill of getting lost.

My mind wanders, so if the topic of how close I am to my mother comes up and I'm at a loss for words, it's not because I have anything bad to say, it's because I wish she understood nobody could ever fill her shoes. When she walked out, it left quite the bear trap. I took her maiden name but I would have preferred her blessings for when I tie the knot. Chokes me up when women mention they're "the type you take home to mom" but they don't know that door's been closed.

Cast away. Like my sister. Since my mother was diagnosed with schizophrenia, she's cleared her apartment of all the pictures of us. And though I've tried to compartmentalize that pain, I can't help but wonder if I showed up unannounced at her doormat, which woman I would see? The woman who used to kiss me on my forehead and call me Jeremy Michael? The woman who would try to lure me into bed with her without clothes? The woman who called the cops on me days before my high school graduation because I stood up for my father when she said I was just like him? Or the woman who told me earlier this year how much of herself she sees in me?

Truth is, I should be thanking her. It was her at the abortion clinic when her family told her that she wouldn't finish high school as a teenage mom. So for her bravery, for walking out, she passed with flying colors. She didn't need a diploma to graduate from hard knocks and although her side of the family always treated me like the black sheep, she never sat back and allowed me to get fed to the wolves. Had my hair dripping with jheri curl juice with a hand full of ceviche at every Thanksgiving. She never could afford presents under that Christmas tree but I felt giftwrapped every time she held me.

When welfare gave her the bare minimum, she intentionally taught me how to give thanks for everything because I knew what nothing felt like. And when teenagers taunted her at Burger King for mopping floors, she subconsciously placed a crown on my head because I almost handed out royal ass whoopings, but learned how mighty a weapon the sword is and a King doesn't spar with peasants. And when I inherited her stutter as a child and went through grade school being teased, instead of blaming her I should have thanked her for enrolling me in the life course called resiliency.

I should be the one apologizing for showing how spoiled I was when she couldn't purchase Fubu jerseys at the commissary, so she put it on layaway. For showing up at her place with my grandmother's maiden name tatted on my forearm. I know why she was so short spoken because it had to feel like a punch to the gut. For being embarrassed by how she couldn't help with my homework in middle school and all the other parents could. For those Betty Crocker meals that never filled me up but how much of her wallet she cleared out to put dinner on the table.

I compared her to everyone else. And she failed. Now, as her hair falls out and her medication picks up, the person I used to see as the victim doesn't exist in the mirror anymore. You think your parents are supposed to be perfect when you're young, but as you grow you see how they made wine out of water.

How a scrapbook can feel like the New Testament. How baby teeth look like a hidden treasure. How every finger painting looks like Picasso. How every saved letter looks like autographed memorabilia. How on their will and testament, your name looks like an acceptance letter to Hogwarts. And then it hits you. None of us are getting out of here alive. How magical it must be to forgive.

It's been hard on my relationships. Searching for you in every woman that I meet. Maybe that explains why I like crazy. But I had a dream we danced at my wedding. My father was there too, and for once in my life, I looked in a room and saw my past and my future had finally called a truce with each other. All those growing pains were exonerated. Time had finally healed all wounds. I didn't feel like an orphan anymore and instead of sending you to a retirement home, I allowed you to move in with my new family. I changed your diapers the way you did mine and pushed your wheelchair the same way you did my stroller and I gave my daughter your middle name so when you're gone, this love would continue until the end of time. But then I woke up. And years later, maybe later than it should've been, the lights finally came on.

17 | Fifty Shades of Grey

It's the greatest burden other than writing. Manhood.
Run far away from anyone telling you what men are hardwired to do. Manhood isn't some monolithic thing that we all fit under.

It would seem, from my experiences, women are taught somewhere early, maybe in elementary school, to use the rhetorical phrase, "Be a man." Usually to incite us or attack our lack of demonstrated masculinity. Almost like they're taken one by one out of the classroom and placed in designated classes for an intensive training on the perfect timing of how to use it in conversations or arguments.

When going out to eat, as a man, you must know what to order because women hate indecision and by definition, men are supposed to be decisive. When courting a woman on a date, men are supposed to pay the entire bill because it shows initiative. Women love that. When shopping for the opposite sex, men are supposed to provide and since diamonds are a woman's best friend, you can just start to hum your favorite retail diamond store commercial [here]. When working out, I need to be lifting twice my weight, grunting, drinking protein shakes because nobody wants a

69

sissy on the treadmill, drinking a vanilla latte. When grooming, I should grow a beard because nothing says masculinity like finding crumbs in there for later, but could you really judge me if I said I do all of these to fit into society's standard of "being a man." When I googled "manly characteristics," about 1000 search pages came up; a variety ranging from "the art of manliness" to "why women love men that are assholes."

When asked what it takes to be a man, everybody's answer varies. Women have told me, "grow some balls," others "take control," and occasionally "stop being a pussy." It does strike me as rather peculiar in every scenario. The truly most fascinating part about being called a pussy is how contradictory that word is. Those things can take a pounding.

In both phases of my life, childhood and manhood, it seems as if there were 50 shades of Grey. I have tried to demonstrate "manhood" in every phase of my life. The problem is I believe it to be too intertwined with "masculinity" which comes with its own stereotypes and robustness. Obviously, since the invention of the phrase "girly man" by California's most famous governator, if you exhibit anything less than Rambo testosterone you fit into this category.

We'll all see a football game, but what's more entertaining than the actual sport (which I love) are the commercials. You ever count how many erectile dysfunction ads they have in the course of that 3-hour span? I counted once. 30. Imagine the Super Bowl. Heaven forbid, you lack the ability to form an erect penis before sex, or mid sex you catch a limp one. What that would do to your masculinity? Well luckily, that's happened to me. More than once. Do I need Viagra? Probably not. However, we see all the places that conversation can turn.

It would be impossible to think anyone when told to "be a man," would have the same response as another, but it's something worth thinking about. At least from the perspective of the person asking. If you need to remind someone to be one, maybe you do us all a favor and create a YouTube video demonstrating how. That would save us all a lot of time struggling with the answer.

18 | Chopping Block

I've been searching for you in every man that I meet. Unintentionally flexing my wit so they could be impressed enough to select me as their first round draft pick. I don't recall sitting on top of broad shoulders that felt like twin towers, but I would wager my retirement plan that it was the best seat in the house.

I'd refund every relationship I ever forged for one father and son backyard bonding experience over George Foreman Grills, so I wouldn't feel so shortchanged. Anything to get me off the chopping block. 'Cause I been in the same spot ever since you left. All my other classmates have been authorized to make that trip, but you were too busy playing the field so my general permission slip is still blank.

Absent. So technically you never failed at anything except letting me down, but you didn't leave enough of a presence for me to move forward. So as a result I've been forced to repeat that lesson every year. Yearning for that stamp of approval. No wonder the wound hasn't sealed.

Spent your days chasing waterfalls, avoiding the lakes and the rivers I had to swim upstream through. I was shark bait. Almost lost a fin. You could've braved your way past all odds to locate me but you were never one for adventure. Maybe you suffered from short-term memory loss because you never remembered me.

But that didn't stop Marlin from finding Nemo. Go fish. So at school I got clowned. I wanted so desperately to run into your arms on those "bring your hero" to class days even if your hands were empty so that you could feel rich. To hear you brag about me at a track meet or on back to school nights like "that's my boy," would have been the greatest gift I could have ever received.

Rest in Peace Uncle Phil. Closest thing to a father that I ever knew. Crazy how 30 minutes was an entire middle passage for such an impressionable mind. Felt he had joint custody the way he picked me up when I was down and brought me to Bel Air.

I was having trouble in my neighborhood, but no matter how many times I whistled, that cab never came. So instead, life stayed flipped upside down. When the credits rolled, the remainder of my story stayed upside down. Grandma taught me how to shoot hoops with one hip so I had to work extra hard on my pivot.

Sophomore year of college, my boss's girlfriend showed me how to tie my tie before the interview so I keep a well tailored suit because it's good etiquette and she told me it is to women what lingerie is to us.

"Are you my mother?" My favorite children's book by Dr. Seuss because I can relate to looking for answers outta everyone in attempts they'll bring me closer to you since I been out of the nest.

Besides, my autobiography is too painful. I'd rather view the world from a different page.

It used to take a massive leap for anyone to get over my pride rock. Or maybe it was the chip on my shoulder. Thank you. I credit you for its construction. I had to retrieve some of the barbwire you left when you fenced me out for the chimney because I never cared for anyone popping in and out of my life once a year.

Detaching myself is exhausting. The problem with withholding yourself from others is after long enough you'll no longer be able to feel anything and I'd rather feel chills every time I hear Mufasa roar. Even if I personally didn't disobey him, I wanted to know what it sounded like to hear a father who cared.

I would've wandered to the elephant graveyard daily just to experience being punished by a father figure than to have my mother pay bail because she taught me everything, but how to be a man. I needed that alpha male and while I did figure out this whole circle of life, you left quite the scar.

I never had a rightful place to the throne so like many abandoned cubs we spend our lives running around stray. Begging to be adopted into a society we were forced to adapt to. Instead of breaking the cycle we escape away from responsibilities and never look back. Hakuna matata. Because it's hard to go from fatherless to fatherhood.

I've had to go back to the drawing board because I've been unsuccessful in finding your heir. It's difficult to find a stern, but concerned surrogate to impart lessons about sex, drugs, violence, and the plight of the young black man in America.

Cuba didn't know how good he had it in that film. I would've traded my room in the suburbs to be one of the Boyz in the the Hood, if I could've had Furious' style. Popular Opinion: I didn't have a father and look at me now, I made it. Unpopular Opinion: But I shouldn't have had to.

There is no force more powerful than someone determined to rise, but there is no replacement for being touched by a wanting pair of masculine hands. I call every older man I meet sir and I can't tell you the triumph I feel whenever they address me as "son."

I wish I never picked up the phone when you called collect, so I wouldn't be haunted by the sound of your voice. Got a ton of pain in your heart this world could never begin to understand so it doesn't reduce the ache when they call you deadbeat.

It mattered you didn't tell me I looked handsome on my first picture day because although dramatic, all I saw was you in my first mug shot. I never told anyone that. My eyes swell anytime I pronounce your name. I can barely get the syllable out without choking.

And when I think about that time I got jumped, I can't help but confess that out of nowhere, I thought you would jump out. Just wanted to be saved so badly by the one person I knew who was a superhero, but didn't believe in his own powers. After all these years I still haven't given up on you. Actually, I'm positive. Even on my sickbed you'll come rescue me like they all do in all the comics.

19 | I Had No Idea You Were So Well Spoken

Thank you for the backhanded compliment. You were better off offering a left hook. That way I would've been out of commission, but instead, you opened up Pandora's Box. With shade like that, I feel on my patio so we might as well roll behind the woodshed. That's code for take your ass to church.

You misinterpret the syntax of my melanin. You're used to catching the ABC evening news where producers tactfully broadcast journalists in the hood with the most illiterate of us for views. In context, I am not the one. If you were expecting a rapid flow of ebonics to avalanche outta my mouth you are misunderstood. Instead let me reenact a scene from Exodus and part your mind of its ignorance. Its bliss is in drought. Free you of enslavement like Moses did the Israelite. See, this ain't no Red Sea, but you might learn to look both ways before crossing me.

You offend me. Such closed minds should be closed for business. I have encountered my fair share of fair-skin colleagues, who have been thrown off guard while inadvertently throwing me under the bus. Recognizing, I too, am equally qualified isn't quantum physics. Putting me on the spot won't get me to shuck n' jive. Your firm beliefs of division based on race has been socially constructed. So allow me to wipe the slate clean. I was taught to speak grammatically correct because I was told I have to work twice as hard just to get half as far and since I am here today, it is proof I paid attention. Respect my conglomerate.

When I speak, I pronounce every syllable. When I got teased because I couldn't speak without stuttering, I spent weekends head over heels on them hooked on phonics videos. When I got punked on the regular for "talking white" at inner city schools, the writer in me must have become an arsonist because I wanted to set the world on fire. Harriet didn't take 19 trips on the Underground Railroad so I could sit in the back of every english class quoting Niggas With Attitude. That kind of thinking has us living minimum wage while waging war on each other. Killing your own ain't gangsta.

Call me square, but I saw myself in a doctor's bonnet even when teachers made me wear that dunce cap. Pardon me if I can't openly accept your compliment. Throwing supercilious words at me won't warrant a response. You don't fear the thug at the corner store, you fear the black man in the corporate world. Here he is. I'll shoot you an email after the meeting, after I'm done packing for next week's retreat. Give me a blunt evaluation of my performance if you're my supervisor. Otherwise, your two cents won't fill my gas tank. In the meantime, here's a penny for your thoughts.

20 | This Kind of Love

Ain't made for everyone. Type to give ya Goosebumps, cure the hiccups, lower fevers, raise standards. You were a big hug on a bad day, how you provided strong lungs for an asthmatic, taught a dyslexic to write abstract, showed an infant with speech impediments he could give speeches at college commencements, is unprecedented. How you worked two full time jobs, but still made time on weekdays to attend soccer practice, showed me as a pipsqueak the gigantic heights that love could reach.

No. This kinda love ain't made for everyone. When I cried on holidays about missing my parents, you never told me to wipe away those tears. You made me channel them. I might have felt periods of abandonment, but I never felt inadequate. I was special (or so you said) so I couldn't ignore it. Used to suffer from night terrors before you took full custody. A love like this had to be made of concrete because when you rocked me, I just felt so safe at night. My dream catcher.

Yeah this kinda love, ain't made for everyone. When I used to be insecure about smiling because I had buck teeth, you didn't hesitate to put my butt in braces and on those days I didn't wanna crack a smile, you made me laugh. When acne made those prom pictures hard to face, you had no problem cooking up home remedies that made it easier to look in the mirror. I might've been picked on in grade school or picked last at recess, but even when I picked at myself, you could pick up all the stuffing and put me back together.

See this kinda love ain't made for everyone. You unbandaged those scars I tried to hide from the world. Filled my spirit when the emptiness to my rabbit hole had no floor. Had the sins of my father and my mother's insecurities. So when I couldn't stand myself, you taught me how to kneel. Can't tell you how many evenings Colossians kept me off the streets, but I can tell you how many times I prayed for strength and you would cover me like banners hanging in the rafter. I can do anything. You said that. And you meant that. I thank you. I don't know where I'd really be without that.

Your love wasn't made for everyone. So I made sure to reward you with the highest form of flattery, imitation. When doctors diagnosed you and left you with months to live, we watched decades fly by. Toasted every New Year's Eve with cider 'til I was of age for champagne. Wheeled you around like you were on a stroller again on that Las Vegas Strip when Celine Dion was on tour. Rocked you to sleep during those cold dialysis treatments. Caught every one of those warm tears on my cheek when cancer took your breast. Tatted your wings on my chest when gangrene snatched your feet and in spite of it all, we claimed victory before we ever considered calling it quits.

Our kinda love can't be made for everyone. The older I've gotten, the more I've realized how I'm not for everyone. I love too abundantly. I take things too personally. I speak too candidly. I live too openly. I don't know how to hold back. I have a hard time fitting in. I struggle with keeping it to myself. I refuse to walk away. Met a lot of people who don't have the conditioning to love intensely, from personal to universal, but most of all unconditionally.

I wish I could tell you things haven't changed since you've been gone but you're still the voice I carry. Your likeliness will be in the woman I marry. Every hummingbird I see reminds me you're still keeping an eye on me. I intend on loving you as much as I did in pampers until the day I'm in dentures. So every birthday of yours that passes, do you think I could ever not add another love letter to your collection? Still as much involved in my life in the afterlife as you were after school. That is one thing that will never change. This kinda love isn't made for everyone because everyone doesn't believe in miracles.

Tender

21 | Thick Everything

Thick waist, thick eyebrows, thick lips. Thick maple syrup on my pancakes, thick everything. Thick hips, thick bacon, thick accents. Thick whipped cream all over my banana split. Thick everything. Thick skin, thick font, thick blankets. Thick nail marks down the side of my back. Thick everything.

Think twice before you mud sling any substance other than flattery. Thick knit onesies for all the men that ever slept on you because they were under the false pretenses that too much of anything is bad.

Thick spine. Excellent because I'm eager to manipulate your body of content. Licking the tip of my index before I turn each page so your words can stick to me. Like every time I see the letter C it reminds me of your butt because it's big and arched and no matter how many squats you do, it doesn't get smaller, it gets rounder.

Have you ever tried to squeeze a bombshell in a pair of skinny jeans? Me neither. Show me side by side before and after pics and the only progress I'll find is how society has created an optical illusion by atmospheric conditions to force you to believe it's possible to look better as a human mannequin.

Mirage. It's not practical or possible for an everyday woman to lack cellulite. You were created to be voluptuous, not to keep count of carbs. Each pound could be measured in gold. You don't come in sample size or proportion. Your temple should be accentuated; you're not a pole tent.

Never been a fan of bathroom scales. Metric systems that only scale back insecurities. Just an effective torture device like the guillotine. Not to gas you up but when you step on the sidewalk, squares glow. And you don't need to ask me how I know because once you passed by I damn near broke my neck trying to get the full picture.

Your type of benevolence should require a disclaimer the way you keep me returning. Missing person signs taped to trunks of magnolia for all the lost souls blood hounds couldn't track once they realized how much heat was being emitted trying to start a fire with twigs.

I'd like to think of you as some artifact out of the renaissance. Of course without the corsets. You would be on a chapel ceiling next to Venus of Urbino. Preeminent next to any postmodern cover model. I like my mural thick. Undiluted and imperfect just the way GOD intended.

Skip the guilt trip people pay you and enjoy your voyage. Release that cargo. You may very well be of "ample proportions" or "well upholstered," but save all explanations. People are naturally shallow, so they'd never understand big words. Take it from Moby Dick; you were built for speed and comfort.

Do you know how many songs have been written about you? If you could only be as happy in your own skin as my ears are anytime Baby Got Back comes on. Your thunder thighs are so sexy they literally can't stop touching each other. Your stretch marks symbolize lightning strikes. The simple reminders Mother Nature left that you can weather any storm.

22 | Chink in the armor

I'm not the guy for you. But I'd like to be. To be next to me is to be next to fire and falling in love with me can only lead to spontaneous combustion. I've watched it. Taken the most levelheaded women and brought them to the brink of insanity.

I'm good at bringing the madness out. It doesn't take a lot of soul searching. You might find someone preferable for your parents, but never someone who plays better with your monsters.

You have a type I don't fit. You like 'em 6'4, chocolate coated, clean cut, straight-laced, white collared, and 6 figured.

I'm more of a 5'10, caramel macchiato, No-Shave-November, blazer and v-neck, black power, work my fingers to the bone and use whatever's left to write about the skeletons in my closet type of guy.

But I'd rather be the anomaly than follow the protocol. There's a reason your knights have never provided a fairy tale ending. That's why I'm fine being the chink in the armor.

I want to put you on the Mount Rushmore of figures that I have engraved on my heart. Next to God, next to my grandma, and my niece. But it wouldn't be my goal to freeze you like a statue because you're better in motion.

I adore the slope of your chest. Savor the curve of your hips. Bask in the proportion of your backside. Every crease that is unequivocally yours. The scars that pull up a chair among small talk where coffee meet bagels. The freckles that dance across your collarbone like constellations or the ones that travel from cheek to cheek like meteoroids.

I wish I had more hours on the clock to wind up the courage to explain how I've never met someone who understands how I tick without giving them a hand. But even time was in love with you, so I understand why it was always rushing and flying whenever you were near. My delorean is parallel parked in case you want to rewind time and experience what our grandparents had; to then travel back to the future to see how even when your hair turns grey you'll still have me floating on air.

Modestly speaking, I've already fed you sex, science, and spirituality.

I know your covers still reek of my scent and your pillows have moans saved within the cases. Do you hear my pleasure in ya sleepless nights? Whatever made your eyes roll back into that perfect place of spontaneous blackness to the cries that come out the places you forgot existed. From the salt in the sweat of your back to the sweet taste of orgasms in the morning, the only thing you've straddled is my face or my lap, never a line of ambiguity.

Do I have to spell it out for you or scream it from the top of my lungs? The chemistry between us could destroy this place. You must possess golden gloves how you catch my sarcasm without breaking a sweat. In our own world when we're in public. At times I'm extra, but together we're extraterrestrial. How amazing it is to find someone who wants to hear about all the things that go on in your head.

I still remember the nights you blessed yourself in my arms. The god in you sent the demons in me running soon as you gave me a temple like yours to worship. Lost in our pillow talk, finding the best parts of our deceased loved ones in one another. Undergoing out-of-body experiences the deeper I travel down your rabbit hole. Falling asleep on your uterus, I could've died like this. Buried alive with my faith renewed. Your initials written on my sarcophagus.

I hope you like them bold, assertive, and tender all at the same time 'cause that's what I am. Chaos of thought and emotion, whirlwind of feelings you wouldn't know you wanted until you had it. I'm not a safe bet. My past isn't a sure thing. But if you value the authenticity of a moment, that's a service I can provide because I doubt you'll be touched by a pair of more wanting hands. Or kissed like someone was drowning and you were air. I know you feel something from just our gaze. This connection opens a gateway to realization and in that discovery; you'll find my quiet comfort.

It can be unsettling at first but that's the most beautiful paradox of it all. How the human heart is heartbreakingly fragile and unshakably strong at the same time. When's the last time you witnessed the firepower of it fully armed and operational?

We beg women to love themselves but tell confident women to calm down. How many men felt their light dimmed by yours? Ever wonder why things always felt so black and white with your previous relationships? They never saw you out of the box they put you in. If there's one thing I'm good at, it's bringing color wherever I go. Maybe all along what you needed was me to complete the picture.

23 | Muse

I've been doing a lot of core work lately. In attempt to tone up my midsection to have the guts strong enough to tell you what I think. I'm still working on that part, but I can tell when I read your words, someone taught their daughter to be worried less about fitting into glass slippers and more into shattering glass ceilings.

My doctor recommended bifocals because I've had trouble lately focusing on small things since I started going on binge readings of your blog. I take that as a good sign. You fuse metaphors like a florist. I wish you could tell me which part of yourself you hated the most so I know exactly where to plant my lips every time I saw you.

I started looking at community colleges just so I can take a course on human anatomy to help me better understand when I see your heart lying vulnerable in your writing, how you sleep with it outside of your chest. It's just unfathomable how you strip away the veil of familiarity and lay elegantly bare amongst passing strangers with a lifted conscience.

I had to learn the Heimlich for when you get too deep to help me maneuver. Whenever I backstroke into your brain waves, I float across your English Channel. Weak swimmers get washed ashore. It's my daily routine to scroll through your body paragraphs. No matter how long I'm in your neck of the woods, I always return with something to think about at my headboard. Divide ya wisdom into morning inspiration and afterthoughts. They're the first thing that touch me in the morning and the last thing I taste at night.

It got to the point where I had to buy a fan to fall asleep. It's no mystery that you find yourself in my wet dreams. Intelligence is the ultimate aphrodisiac so even when I'm nocturnal, you stream my libido. Your equilibrium got me grabbing bed sheets. Telepathically, got me speaking in tongues. Got me pondering bondage after bedtime. Fishnet stockings. Thigh high boots. Got me waking up to my feet tied in suspender belts. Quite the Dominatrix. You didn't have to wake my neighbors to reawaken me.

I can only imagine how many undeserving men have lacked the sobriety to walk your line of thinking. I take water breaks throughout compound sentences every time you write about love because I cramp up. Your adjectives remind me how painful it can be. It's like I get shin splints anytime I feel symptoms that I'm falling again, but I enjoy a good cliffhanger. You've uprooted the planted schemes of what connection means. I bet you have questions like, "Where did you come from?" The most noteworthy thing is you attract what you're ready for. And I'm here.

24 | Twenty-Four Hours

If I had 24 hours until I self-destructed, could I go all bombs away with you?

I'd like to observe fireworks to adequately reflect the display of flames your vehicle of affection propels when our lips explode on contact.

The quintessential explosive pyrotechnic.

If you studied me closely, I would hope I'd display the kind of emotions that would be hard to get a hold of among regular table settings.

Ever since my ex left me feeling like damaged goods, I've had to rely more on my gut instinct and less on heart to heart because those exchanges can get lost in the universe. So if I seal myself off, it's only to see if you possess the type of care package to address me.

If I shed light on these blind spots, could you see me for what I am?

I don't need you to make me feel complete, but having these wounds kissed by someone who doesn't see them as disasters to my soul, but cracks to put their love into, is the most calming thing in this world.

I'm the kind of mathematical equation that doesn't add up, but I'm hoping my words are calculated enough to make you feel twice the person you are without you having to divide your legs.

I have a tendency when I eat food to get crumbs lost in my beard. Could you find yourself willing to lick your finger like a motherly figure and withdraw it from the crevice of these lips without a cordial invitation? Or is that the kind of love you'd consider weird?

Highly questionable how you provide the perfect remedy to my sore throat and tongue by simply helping me swallow my pride.

The signs are everywhere. How you overcame these vertical walls, tunneling your energy by taking a liking to finding your way under my transparent ceiling.

How many trials did it take to be hungry enough to run my maze even when I rat myself out without a reward in sight because you know how to make me cheese?

You come to me at night in my dreams so it'd be impossible to ask you to skip rocks when picking my brain like cotton albeit you're constantly jumping the fence. Losing sleep when I have to look forward to you. Herding these thoughts. Just counting sheep.

Bottomless mimosas over conversation with sunnyside eggs perfectly well done. We're equally yoked. I love when you keep the dialogue golden and runny.

I pride myself on having good taste in character and you are a fine example of not having to walk on eggshells because you stir my senses.

You're a hearty splash of food for thought, tender from top to bottom and even though there's crust around the edges, you're still tantalizing to my taste buds.

I fuck with you for a variety of reasons, but more than anything else because you helped me discover my ability to want. Like, what kind of man wakes up and rolls over without wanting to walk this tightrope?

I'm wired up. Acrobatic. Balancing these emotional needs and physical lusts. Don't you know how suspended in the air you have me?

My first heartbreak didn't come from the hands of a loved one, but by the cusps of expectations. Cuffed by the thrill of what you offer but unbound by your raw potential.

Up all night making love songs. Complex to think we could provide an excellent backdrop through the sacred art of making your spine curl despite the ability my tongue has to keep you straight on your back.

You're the adventurous type and I enjoy it when you're up to mount my amusement. Park yourself on this hard wood. Hope you don't mind vertical loops. Hooking up these cable cars because we're on the same track, rolling my r's like coasters. Don't mean to keep you waiting in line; you definitely meet the height requirements to enjoy this ride.

Teasing out things in me that I never knew existed. Defibrillator. How much time has elapsed since I hit snooze before you sent that strong electrical shock to my heart to reset its proper rhythm. CLEAR.

I would hate for you to feel you forged the man of your dreams, but if you desire broad shoulders to give you a hand with your burdens, while simultaneously carrying you over the threshold, perhaps you'll be sheltered in these arms.

Keeping your body aligned to your true desires, that's practicing good posture. Preventing this inner urge would require me to pretend you're not a calling, but like a moth to a flame, I'm attracted to your bright light.

Dangerously drawn to you while simultaneously drawing out the truth from me. Gotta be in touch with your soul to meet your soul mate. Residing my secrets in your bungalow. I am home.

25 | Bite Marks On My Tongue

You would've made an excellent x-ray tech. You knew exactly what buttons to push. We broke like skeletons, loving to the bone. Developed signs of early carpal tunnel in my wrist because I tore ligaments trying to hold onto the fond memories that kept me nailed down and while there are still bloodstains on my hands, the last thing I want to hear is how I didn't fight hard enough for you.

I washed my hands in muddy water. You left quite some dirt on my name. I could never glamorize being in a wreck. I've had a phobia of getting back in the saddle because of the last person that drove me crazy. Avoid my rearview mirror at all times because you've taught me enough in hindsight. It feels like jaywalking whenever you cross my mind and I hate to yield even when you have the right of way.

I've become a regular at local laundromats just to take my time for a spin. I've traded all my dollars for quarters and even beat the high score on pac man waiting for someone to shake the vending machine hard enough for my sour skittles to drop, but I don't bother making my bed up. Dirty laundry all in my closet. In fact, I even left some strung up in the street. Sometimes I just need to remember the way a t-shirt can hold a scent of skin for weeks until I don't know what plain cotton smells like anymore and don't even want to.

I didn't know how to breathe without you, until I weaned myself off. Our fallout was atomic, destroying anything within a five-mile radius. We had to bomb to finally crater. Just to see how many years of fresh air we forfeited to mask the toxins. The kind of venom we were living with left untreated would've been enough to have a mamba on sick leave. The type of poison we were spitting was so acidic that even a tarantula would've had its legs up in crutches. There's a weird pleasure in loving something so bad that it hurts.

I used to go to scrap yards to collect all the parts necessary to build a spaceship. Maybe a long time ago, in a galaxy far, far away, we made it work. You've been appearing in my dreams a little too often, which means I don't have to ask if you miss me. When forensics takes a look at my autopsy I don't want them to discover bite marks on my tongue from all the things I never said. I'm not bitter, just sad. But the hopeful kind. The kind of sad that just takes time.

Too many of us dance with two people at our weddings... the one we marry and the one we wish we married instead. The goal is to have them be the same person. There was a time I thought you were both. I must've enjoyed the way each stab wound felt until I took the knife from your hands and finally cut the cord. Former Masochist. I was a glutton for punishment. Gluten-free slices in my back. Maybe I dodged a bullet. It still grazed me. Far from bulletproof but I could never allow my wounds to transform me into someone I'm not. Ironically, losing you helped me rediscover my faith because it's a bad religion to be in love with someone who could never love you the way you deserve to be.

26 | You Can't Buy Sunflowers With Food Stamps

I've waited in my fair share of lines to find out first hand but I've never allowed what I can't afford to prevent me from what I can provide. Didn't grow up with a lot so when the stove wasn't on, I learned how to vent. Been traveling on the road less taken for so long I've rummaged through enough front lawns to learn how to leave trails of rose petals that led from doormats to pillow cases. I never got caught trespassing. Hallelujah. Habitual line crosser. Never been afraid of being in touch with my feminine side, but I've always questioned if I'm man enough.

Enough radio listens and you would believe your love was for sale. In any case I wouldn't have what it takes to be the highest bidder. I've been reluctant to admit I'm a cheap date because you deserve gourmet dishes swallowed with champagne I can't pronounce, but I'm really good at using my resources. I'm a bargain shopper. How else I find you? What a steal. I've collected enough coupons to fill a gift basket with goodies and I specialize in roof top views of the skyline or beachside conversations with white wine, if that's what you're into. And if you can't recall the last time you laughed 'til tears fell, I know a bar in San Francisco where we can karaoke until they kick us out.

I don't have an accountant, so I'm counting on the fact you're not expecting me to break the bank to show you I care. If you're impressed with Instagram likes & hash tags then pay my ideas and gestures no thought. You don't want any scrub but if you want a man to spoil you, you gotta be there in the times he can't. I'm willing to scrub every dish in the city counterclockwise to save up enough pennies to spend a day throwing each one of them in a wishing well until one came true. If you don't believe in european folklore or you're not superstitious by nature, we can paddle canoe to the middle of nowhere to get a better view of what's on the horizon.

I don't own private islands. I don't come with hideaways in the Hampton's. But I do have a lot of patience. The kind that had me sleeping in the trunk of my jeep because I had to decide between gas money or books to earn a bachelor's degree, since I wanted to remind my grandmother her words were far louder than any of the voices of doubt in my head. The kind of patience that keeps me up in the middle of the night writing because even though they don't pay the utilities, one day a publisher will view my work and it'll hit the kind of switch that'll light up enough electricity to power the city. The kind of patience that requires me to grow out this beard without cutting my split ends or getting jealous it catches more crumbs than disposable bibs.

I'd like to imagine it feels like an eternity since your first crush passed you a note in class. I can't promise to beat him up, but I can fill up a scrapbook filled with enough things I love about you, so you can treasure the feeling. Not sure if you've ever been taken ice skating, but I know an outdoor rink hundreds of people go to where you'll be the center of my attention. I know an art walk in Los Angeles full of masterpieces we can go to, if I book tickets weeks in advance; and a theme park that offers amateur batting cages at a ballpark price if you wanna swing for the fences. Things are being loved while people are being used. Offering a rich perspective to the miseducation of materialism. I'm willing to go on a scavenger hunt to help you find all the feelings you've been neglected of.

27 | North Star

I pray you never fall in love with someone, again, who gives you butterflies. Such susceptible and nimble little things. Those fragile wings that once torn, cannot repair themselves. No, I hope the person you adore doesn't entrust you with such delicate invertebrates that lack the boundless three-dimensional extent of surviving love strong enough to cover the continuum of the moon and back like you so adequately deserve.

I've made a horrible zookeeper in my past. Leaving starving caterpillars to hang themselves long enough to morph into adult moths I had no intention to meadow. Netting them as a collector's item. Unaware I was damaging their larva for someone else to mend. Cowardly of me to awaken them once they latched on, without the full disclosure I would come out of my cocoon too.

But you possess the type of magic that drapes the weak. It takes thick skin and fortitude to love a woman of your genetic code. It's in your DNA to multiply what you are given and lukewarm effort isn't something you are capable of reciprocating. You simply don't deserve any sentiment that might come undone at the slightest touch. You should float on clouds so high, from a touch so strong, that Delta Airlines should reward you with frequent flyer miles for all your astral traveling.

You merit someone who makes you feel earthquakes. Something terrifyingly strong to bulldoze those great walls you spent guarding from people like me. Life altering, shaking that reinforces your beliefs system that anyone can rearrange their life to accommodate you in it. A seismic force that rocks you to your inner core. Something summoned from so deep of another you have to stop, drop and roll because love, when done correctly, is urgent. And in case of emergency, you should break these glass ceilings. Something that upheaves you so greatly it has the potential to initiate volcanic activity starting a fire in you that will never die.

I hope in GOD's green and vast, beautiful earth you purposely disobey the GPS and go off road. See what adventures await outside of your comfort zone. Give the chance to someone who is infatuated with you that isn't "your type." Too much time spent with lovers who aren't obsessed. Since you have work around the clock there shouldn't be an hour you aren't reminded how they would turn the hands back if there was a chance to find you sooner. Have the kind of sex that feels so strongly connected that when they get up to use the bathroom early in the morning, it has you sleep walking outside on your balcony because you misinterpreted the sunrise for their body heat.

Your phone should ring at 2 am. Enough to wake you out of the blue to make a brown girl like you blush because those hours exist for lovers and writers and your lips have the ability upon contact to transform anyone into a poet. The fact you spend hours racing through someone's mind should be incentive enough not to drop the baton. The brain has too many tabs open late at night for your line not to be in service. I've accumulated enough notes on you to understand you deserve better. I've accounted for enough of my bad habits to do better. You are a Queen. Don't let no man half love you.

We're just renting out these celestial bodies. When's the last time you held your eyelids open a little longer before you blinked to sort out the stars you felt from another's gaze? You deserve to be shook up so hard someone must look inside you to find the improbability of themselves. Magic 8 ball. Following your drinking gourd to escape how much of me I've enslaved due to pride. Mastering these emotions. Dying a free man. Your north star is liberating.

28 | Sentimental Mood

I love that you believe in me, but I hate that I can let you down so easily. These words are your sun and moon, but my actions are the sea and land they revolve around. You consume every message. Sensitive so they move your mountains. When my temperature rises, there's a high chance of precipitation. Even when my family cut me off for growth to begin, you branched out and kept me rooted. When mistakes and depression became my daily dosage, you were just what the doctored ordered.

You've never questioned my character. You always answered my prayers. You've become so good at patting the dust off my shoulders every time I come out the lion's den. You console the human in me. You control the monster in me. The no-good that can't do-right doesn't have to run away because you always tag along. It's like the greatest blessing to know someone loves you unconditionally without obligation. How you've been so clutch when I've been so clumsy. Keep my head on my shoulders when I've pulled the hairs off from above it.

Me with all these abandonment issues. You with your adaptive spirit. Took time for me to learn stability. Used to volatile environments so I always keep my bag packed at the door. Back against the wall. I don't remember being picked up from daycare as much as I do from waiting rooms in the courthouse which is why as a juvenile, I learned how to be prepared to travel. It was you that helped me unpack those bags. You lessened the load, made light of my bundle, so when it was time for boarding, my baggage never weighed us down. You took me up through the turbulence. What journey worth taking isn't turbulent? But I've always been one to question it all. How the wind blows… Murphy's Law… Resurrection… Why do the things that we love the most destroy us in the end? My guess is that nothing lasts forever. Especially this instant. Blink once and it's already a memory. Blink again; it's something that torments. But before my mind takes me off the deep end, you meet me on common ground, 'cause you got my best interest at heart. It scares me how dependent I am.

Burned bridges before. Often due to my fear of dependency. Easier to cut something off fresh before getting attached, but you latched onto me. It's hard to imagine formulating an escape route from this Alcatraz because now I'm a prisoner of the moment. Ironic how I used to get anxiety by looking ahead too much. My heart is where it needs to be. So both our hearts beat like a metronome, which explains why I'm in a sentimental mood.

Closest I've ever come. That's what you are. Farthest thing from perfect. That's what I am. Opened up chambers I never knew came attached. You teased out things in myself I didn't know existed. Mopped those dirty corners of myself I used to tiptoe over. Departmentalized those flashbacks my counselors tried to diagnose. Tried to give you detours every time you asked me to come clean. The janitor to my soul. How do you deliver me from myself, but hold me to the fire?

Making a diamond from the ashes. You're an anomaly and it feels good not to be wandering aimlessly any longer. I have looked at you in millions of ways and I have loved you in each. If I had my life to live again, I'd find you sooner.

29 | Zero Hour

At first impression, I thought we picked up in the middle of where we left off in our last lifetime. Instrumental how you stream my URL. Did you Google search or are you feeling lucky the way you finish my sentences?

I can tell your first blood didn't come from between your legs, but from biting your tongue. People had to pull teeth to get info out of me because I was never straightforward either but that stems from trying to force something that never sprouted and in this case, I'm willing to spill the beans 'cause your aura seems giant enough to climb.

Can I confess my right foot is smaller than my left? So if I can't walk in a straight line periodically, understand I suffer from a deficiency that doesn't make it better that I'm clumsy when I stumble into my feelings.

Off the record if my house was on fire and I could only grab one thing before the roof came down, it would be grandmother's urn. I made a promise I would return her ashes to her birthplace and a carnival in the West Indies makes for a pretty good homecoming.

Would it make your skin crawl if I recalled the time I thought my chaperone was going to molest me the night before my oratorical competition? I would've chose that lobby floor over the double bed in hindsight if I'd known I'd get no sleep fending my hide when he asked if I needed a room.

Behind closed doors, if I confessed it's the nightmares of all the at-risk youth who've let me peek behind the blinds of a broken home, which I've tried to mentor that keep me up at night, would you keep yours locked?

If I admitted I received a pink slip for spending my lunch money on all the kids who came to my class malnutritioned and didn't follow the script because I was listening to my heart, would my judgment draw red flags?

Confidentially, would I ruin the mood if I asked you to slow dance with me in a room that's so still the only beat is our pulse? I'm impulsive even though I have rhythm like I was born with two left feet and sometimes I like to tap the ground just to remind the devil he hasn't won.

Don't breathe a word, but you'll see the good health that comes with being around you. You've got a body that curves and a mind that stretches for miles. Every time I laugh, I feel it in my abdomen and if you asked, I would say, I have a gut feeling our convos are insanity and with our train of thought, I like the chances of everything working itself out.

Light a sage for zero hour because everything that came before it, is different from everything that comes after. Cleansing the room of all the small talk that was never well suited for you to address before me. Breaking the memory bank wide open. Endless substance withdrawals.

Keeping our discussions of atoms, death, aliens, favorite positions, meaning of life, faraway galaxies, coincidence or. Fate, The Bay or LA, music that makes you feel different, lies your teacher told, astrology signs and compatibility, how we didn't meet sooner, where you'd be if it wasn't for the one who you thought was the one, all the emotions from our dark twisted fantasies, private.

Between you, and me I really honor the "I've never told anyone this" type of conversation. I'm addicted to them. Meeting of the minds. I've used your mental floss between the cracks of myself I didn't know had an opening and I can't forget the flavor.

My lips are sealed when it comes to your learning curve that accompanied being 21. The scars that makeup can't cover could never make me view you any differently. It just reminds me you were stronger than whatever tried to hurt you and what you see as imperfection I consider a representation of your ability to overcome anything that stands in your way.

I could travel to every foreign country on the map to fill your living room with native masks and they still wouldn't equal the countless times I've had to disguise myself for the amusement of others. I left my camouflage at the door when I wiped all the mud I've been dragging my feet in on the mat.

Could you keep it a secret that my list of regrets has become as long as a red carpet and if I rolled it out with everyone I haven't made peace with, are you willing to outbid all of my demons if I auction off some of my broken pieces? I'm hopeful you can bear this pain without breaking.

Never been good at chain of command, but there's a chain reaction anytime your eyes water recounting how you became the skilled sailor you are by overcoming the most stormy seas. You have me tasting the salt of the ocean. You walked the plank blindfolded, look how that panned out. How you battened down the hatches without abandoning ship has me hooked.

I believe in spirit animals like I believe in a Shaman and how the world wouldn't have it's oldest healing tradition without each other. Looking inside of your soul, I found gold and not the gold plated kind, either. It's hard locating the parts of ourselves we concealed in places during hide and seek that we never went back to find.

How the landscape of our conversations has so much in common with the surface of the moon. It's hard for me to let people in, but you opened a wormhole. I trusted the vibes you sent. So I sent them back. You kissed my 3rd eye. Now you're all up in my visions. We have the potential to make beautiful things.

30 | Last Call for Sapiosexuals

You couldn't help me keep it up even if Pixar let you borrow all the balloons from "Up." You couldn't get me hard if you beheaded Medusa with the sword of Perseus and forced me upon her gaze. You couldn't get me erect if you spiked my Jack and Coke with an overdose of Viagra. There is no scenario where I could possibly end up sexually attracted to you because every time you open your mouth, you turn me off.

Granted, even though you have the kinda body that reminds me GOD was our creator, you own the kinda mind that even a map couldn't find. Google maps for that matter. I lose all stamina as soon as you fix ya lips to output data that couldn't have been processed. If you put just a little effort into being mentally attractive, you just might be. I wonder if it's a generational gap or if I was really born in a world where I gotta download an app or talk to Siri for some sign of intelligence.

I reside in an era where women would rather be eye candy than soul food. So many rotten apples that I've been leaning towards going Vegan. It's as if every time I log into social media, I want to jump off the tallest building. One quantum leap for technology, one massive delete to social skills. How you have a trail of selfies, but not a train of thought? Your vanity bores me. The theory we evolved from tadpole into imbecile leads me to believe we were better off extinct with the dinosaurs.

I wish I could wear a "Do Not Disturb" sign on my forehead whenever I walk down Melrose. Whoever told you to play dumb did you a disservice. There is nothing sexy about falling off the stupid tree and hitting every branch on the way down. If looks are all you have to offer, then time and gravity will make a fool of you. If you still believe men like their women to be seen and not heard, you are more than welcome to go back to the 50's. Please take with you the first published edition of *Stepford Wives*.

We've let "blonde moments" last lifetimes. Small talk has become a big challenge. I'd rather skydive without a parachute before I watch reruns of Jersey Shore with you. Terminate my subscription to any and all further dates that include us going dutch. You'd lose ya mind trying to understand mine. Your inability to feed my needs has caused a short circuit that you lack the dialect to repair. It is clear that a perfect evening to you consists of selfie sticks, VH1, a black guy who is 6'1 and a cigarette after sex. I can remove at least one variable from this equation: myself.

Maybe intelligence and aesthetic talent are obsolete. I can't help but believe I'm not the only one that yearns for an incisive, inquisitive, insightful, irreverent brain. I want someone for whom philosophical discussion is foreplay. I want to feel commando at all times. Leave my phone on airplane mode while I take you to the mile high club. Go from coach to the cockpit. When I'm done you won't be flying virgin no more.

Smoking weed under star projectors or hot boxing under a pillow fort. Interpreting dreams, all the while getting moist as you slide down each slippery slope. Mentally undressing you mid-antidotes. Straddling your IQ. Blowing out your cerebral. Leaving your head sprung. That is someone who can rub their clit against my mind anytime. Like, if you could read it right now, you'd have an orgasm.

Made in the USA
San Bernardino, CA
12 December 2019